A WALK WITH GOD

A WALK WITH WITH GOD

JAMES WALKUP

XULON PRESS

Xulon Press
2301 Lucien Way #415
Maitland, FL 32751
407.339.4217
www.xulonpress.com

ISBN-13: 978-1-6628-1590-4
Ebook 978-1-6628-1591-1

Table of Contents

Fishing For The Wasted Few

Fishing for the wasted few,
Humility toward God, he taught,
As, only He alone could teach.
In the clothes and manner
Of a shepherd, He lived.
As a carpenter,
He walked the earth.
Fables of truth He spun,
To any who had ears to hear.
The rich and poor alike,
Are our neighbors, He said.

To Him,
Hearing was listening.
He reached beyond,
The eyes of men's minds
And came, to prepare a place
For all, who would live
As He intended,
According to His purpose,
Without guilt or shame,
All as one always,
This has been His plan.

Since the day,
He first breathed air,
Into the dust,
That was to become mankind,
This was
His plan.

Jim Walkup
1978

One

God
created
each
one
of us
created,
He them,
to become
one flesh
together,
joined
yet separate,
two halves,
united,
two parts,
one.

Jim Walkup
10-06-1999

I First Felt Alone
As I Had Come To Pray

my heart cries out
in stillness
as I come to pray

thoughts of time
spent
with you
have slowly washed
away

the lengthening
shadows remind me
of the shortness
of today

my lifetime
is but
a flicker
in eternity

you bring
meaning
to a day

continued

still
the flapping
of the gray
shingles on
a distant
roof
makes
the stillness
of today
hard to tolerate

and
I can't remember
when
I first
felt alone
as
I had come
to pray

Jim Walkup
11-26-1999

Break My Heart

Father
my heart
is on the floor
before
you.

cleanse me
of all
guilt
and sin,
that I
may
stand
humbly
in your sight.

my mind
and
my spirit
are set
only
on what
is pleasing
to you

break my heart
and
renew your joy
within
me.

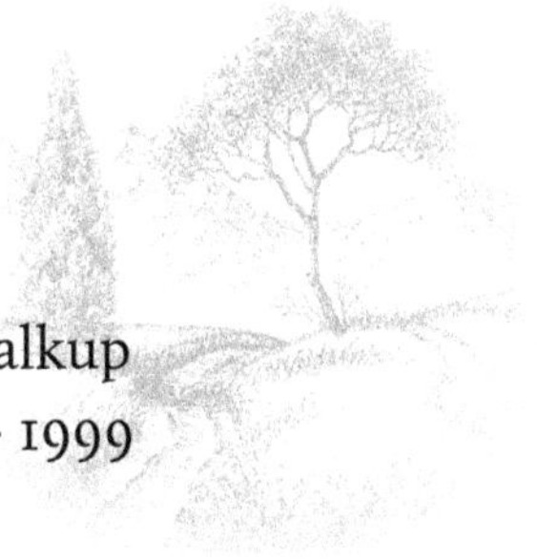

Jim Walkup
11- 26- 1999

Not I But, Jesus

Thought I was living
till He came in,
and Holy Spirit,
gave me a new beginning
Life in death at the Cross.

I was walking in my own strength
and way, when He said
seek first my kingdom
then He began to teach me
His secret of winning,
even though I lose.

I find lately that it's hard
to remember the person
I used to be before His hand
was leading me.

no longer do I need
to fully understand, entirely
His reason or His plan
stated simply
I know that in His time
He's working out
His best in me.

Jim Walkup
11-26-1999

A Happier Face

Perhaps an old horse
is preferable to being horseless
and laughing at yourself
takes you beyond mere acceptance
to the place where battles valiantly fought
have become a relic of the past
and surrender wears a happier face.

Jim Walkup
05-2001

the gypsy lad

pockets full of quarters
a man of purpose
pee coat and derby
the night sang
what's your hurry

a pin ball game
we laughed and thought
time stood still
as we danced the hours till
another day would be
your sad glance
another song
reminder of my friend
the gypsy lad
who used to frolic long

a note
we bid
you to remember
he's laid his bed
quiet
and alone

Jim Walkup
01- 2003

Strength

Every time I hide my face
Every time
I hang my head
Every time
I call his name
Every time
I feel alone
He is with me
He is my Saviour, my Lord
My shelter safe from harm
My comfort comes from Him
and peace amid the storm!
Be still and know
that He is God
Once you've tasted of
his love
the blindness
will be lifted
Thank you Jesus!!
Phil 4:13
"I can do all things through
Him who gives me strength"
Every time I hide my face
Every time I hang my head
Every time I call his name
Every time I feel alone
He is with me
He is my Savior, my Lord
my shelter safe from harm
my comfort comes from Him
and peace amid the storm

Jim Walkup
01- 29- 2003

Every Time I Hide My Face

Every time I Hide My Face
Every time I hang my head
Every time I call His name
Every time I feel alone
He is with me

He is my Savior , my Lord
My shelter safe from harm
My comfort comes from Him
And peace amid the storm!

Jim Walkup
01-29-2003

An Even Keel

When I feel persecuted,
broken,
alone,
He is my shield steadfast,
my courage and strength,
ready to make
my way steady,
upright unwavering,
an even keel
amidst the storm.

Jim Walkup
03- 03- 2004

A place apart

When I'm hungry,
in need,
without a source
of refuge
He is my comfort,
my solace,
a fortress,
my place of rest
He allows me
quiet tranquility
a place apart.

Jim Walkup
03-09-2004

Sharing In Her Joy

In a place of inner peace
Gentle serenity settles on
The place where memories
Are stored and my mind
Feels warmth and ease
Echoing a soft And gentle song
And I'm filled with A realization all day long
living for the moment
Sharing in her inner joy
Thank you Lord Escapes my lips
Echoing a gentle song
A moment of delight
All day long
To be living in Her inner joy.

Jim Walkup
04-22-2004

Laughing Spirit

Memories of a day left
On some canyon wall
a painted desert
shimmering waterfall
little ants scurry
along in single file
what's the reason
why does it rain
on the land so dry
bereft of moisture

Laughing spirit
cloudless sky
pretty rainbows
violet and red
How'd you do it
Answers to questions
All lose their meaning
Thank you God
for another special day
before we ask why

Jim Walkup
06- 22- 2005

Dearest 2

My love cannot find the words to speak
As I realize the softness of your touch.
My heart is aglow as I reach
For your body to close
you in a soft embrace.
My eyes close and my heart beats steady
And my lips find no words to speak.
As our bodies touch in a soft release.

Jim Walkup
09-08-2006

Dearest

I love your sense of humor
and your ability to laugh easily.
I long to touch your soft hand
and not speak a word
whether true or false.
Just to lay near you
and to feel the day
like a burden lifted.
I desire to say it simply
with words like I love you,
allowing the moment
to gently slip away.

Jim Walkup
09-08-2006

Keep Going 2

When I need to believe,
As sometimes
My feet may slip.
It could be as close
As the next step.
But my God is strong and steady
His arms surround, enfold
And bring comfort, strength,
And renewal to my soul.
His words like a light
In my heart, quietly say
I'm with you, hold on
My child, fear not
Keep going.
A song of simple
Joy then fills my mind,
As I continue with my day.

Jim Walkup
10-15-2006

A Moment of Joy

A song in our hearts
a glance, a step
A moment of joy,
with an embrace,
Our faces meet as we share
A moment of bliss a smile,
a tear as we gently kiss.

Jim Walkup
11-11-2006

Child's Radiance

How much is she worth
God has blessed her with beauty
beyond measure.
Her eyes brighten
with a child's radiance
her eyes shine forth as
a smile comes to her face.

Jim Walkup
11-11-2006

Good And Faithful Saying,

1 Timothy 1:15

The saying is trustworthy
and deserving of full acceptance,
that Christ Jesus came into
the world to save sinners,
of whom I am the foremost.
And open your heart in repentance
Then rejoice when people say
What is the difference
Have you given your Heart
To the Lord

Jim Walkup
03-19-2007

It Is Finished

Our God is revealed
in the stars
that light the way home
His spirit shines forth
like a calming peace
amidst a storm
His is the strength that
helps to hold on.
Our Lord is love,
coming to earth
in a physical body
He would suffer,
taking our place
to know how it feels.
Saying at last
it is finished,
My work
is complete.

Jim Walkup
03-19-2007

A Calm Peace

A Calm Peace God is revealed in
the clear blue sky peeking through
every cloud,
the brilliance of
heaven so high and warmth of
the sun's golden rays.
He is speaking through
a mothers' gentle song
singing softly as she sooths a child
sleepy in her hands.
a soft whisper
as the suns light
sweeps over the land.
A day filled with warmth
and new hope awaken
with warmth and a radiant
brilliance, a newness
awaking the day.
Dear Lord,
Our redeemer,
You renew and bring joy
to your child speaking,
while a calm peace
settles the moment,
quietly and serenely,
as he prays.

Jim Walkup
03-19- 2007

My God

You bring the sunshine
And the rain on both the evil and the good.
You that are the bright and morning star,
You that are the beginning without an end.
My Lord, and My God
Thank You for the love and overflowing
joy that you bestow on me
and my life.

Jim Walkup
08-20-2007

There Is A Treasure

There is a treasure
that lies within
the heart of a friend
telling me,
I need not guard
my words and
playfully pretend.

Like a song
of your love
it brings to mind
courageously,
trusting and
reassuring kind
thoughts,
a still small voice

In the heart
with unspoken words
of homage and praise,
and certain cords
of thanksgiving
and devotion,
a treasure
within the heart.

Jim Walkup
01- 31-2008

Love Is Not Blind

Love is not blind.
Love is patient.
Love is kind.
You may timidly ask
why does it seem
such a contradiction,
A song that does not rhyme,
like a resounding gong
or a clanging cymbal,
And now these
three remain,
faith, hope, and love
but the greatest
of these is love.

[After 1 Cor 13:13]

Jim Walkup
02-12- 2008

O' Gentle One

O' gentle one
You bring sunshine
to each moment of the day,
Reminding me
that there is hope,
a reason to find
confidence And believe.

Quietly we pray
and joy comes
In the morning
replenishing, renewing,
anxiety and discouragement
fade away.
They disappear
as quietly we pray.

Jim Walkup
08-27-2008

Look For What Is Sacred

To find happiness
Seek friendship openly.
To find unity
Give what you have freely.
To find joy
Learn to treasure
what is good in others.
To find harmony
look for what is sacred
in the commonplace.

Jim Walkup
11-06-2008

Solitude

It's easier not to see
Than to be invisible,
a shadow of someone
you barely know.

And it's hard at times
to find a reason
to walk in solitude
rather than to live for a time
on simple gratitude.

It seems so amazing
to suddenly catch
a glimpse of eternity,
while climbing up God's
transparent mountain
being seen,
and yet hardly ever
looked upon.

Jim Walkup
11-18-2008

A Brighter Tomorrow

Whether plentiful
or meager fare
my Lord,
my Sustainer,
and Creator
is always there
beside me,
along side me,
always near

when clouds of doubt
seem to be really clear
close at hand,
words in prayer,
silently spoken
reminding me
that my Lord, my God
is also very near.

You are my God,
my redeemer
when in laughter
or in sorrow
you bring promise
to my spirit,
and hope of a
brighter tomorrow.

Jim Walkup
11-19-2008

What Can You Receive

What can you
receive from me,
a thought, a smile
be it ever so small
and insignificant to give,
and yet so easy,
although you may be wanting
nothing more than to return
a glance, or to hold a hand
in silence and gratitude.
Patiently waiting your turn,
internalized moment,
and then to speak,
and humbly take a stand,
some gentle words
seem easy to receive,
a feeling is spoken,
"I forgive you."

Jim Walkup
02-19-2009

Winning

Mine Isn't the best,
It's the first.
But I thought you said,
"the prettiest won."
Still mine isn't
the best or the worst.
So by whose standard
do we judge
what is best,
or who is first.

Jim Walkup
12-24-2009

Something To Treasure

Mary Jo is enjoying her time in Missouri.
And visiting relatives is shared
and blessed experience,
different each day and time
they meet together.
A joy and something to treasure.
As our Lord has gifted her
with beauty beyond measure.

Jim Walkup
06-06-2010

Small Ship

A small ship
sailed by, and the wind,
blew steadily as the boat
swayed and dipped.
Then quietly settled softly
on the shore.
The wind gently buffeted
the little boat,
and silently in the night
the breeze died away.

Jim Walkup
10-30-2013

Gladness (from Isaiah 41: 10)

Dear Lord,
I'm so grateful
that because of you
We don't have to
go it alone.
When I wonder
about the way,
You have gratefully,
given such joy
and gladness,
forgiveness, mercifully,
you care about our longings.
You remove dismay,
and lighten our load
and you take away,
our fear, and provide
help to strengthen us,
Then you patiently uphold
us with your righteous
right hand

Jim Walkup
02-14-2014

Sad Face

It's easy to lose heart
when you ask me to be
close to you
and you leave me
with a sad face.
Then you say you
don't understand why
I appear to be hurt
and yet wisdom says
to give it another try.

Jim Walkup
09-25-2015

His Promises

Life's circumstances
and issues come and go
we ride them like a roller coaster.
But God's love for us
Never wavers
His love shines through
when we put our trust,
and faith in Him,
because His promises
are faithful, and true.

Jim Walkup
02- 09-2016

Truthfulness
And Grace

She required truthfulness
And it captured my heart.
Her and I spoke together
closely from the start
about a friendship,
that would last forever

She smiled and spoke quietly
about a heavenly place
her words caused me to think
of those pearly gates,
the streets of gold,
a new Jerusalem
and an abundant life
of fellowship and grace

Jim Walkup
03-02-2016

What Is Said (Proverbs 16:9)

Who says,
what is said
is more important,
than how it is said,
or who says it.

If Holy Spirit
directs our thoughts
and words
then what is said
is guided by His will,
so the words
that are spoken
are his
not
ours.

Jim Walkup
03-05-2016

Learn of Me 2

In this world
of many voices,
my heart wanted
to do the right thing,
while I grew in
greater understanding.

A voice said listen
to me, my dear
child, and learn,
and grow in knowledge
of Me, and discern
My ways so that
you do not follow
your own ideas,
but walk in a way
pleasing to Me.

Be of good cheer
because I have
overcome the world,
and know that My love
is faithful, and
undiminished
by circumstances.

My God is near
He will grow
and strengthen
you during trials
and tribulations
that beset you.

Jim Walkup
03-14-2016

Value

We need to value
the everyday we took
To be nothing.
Things that we often state
as being of little worth
that are often over looked.
Things which seem insignificant
while they hold great
value.

Jim Walkup
12-29-2016

On My Knees

My desire for the LORD
Is greatly magnified
by my love For Him
joyful moments observed
silently in one accord
time spent on my knees
intercessory moments
of Holy Spirit close beside.

Jim Walkup
01-16-2017

Blessed Beyond Measure

Finding our way in life
Is often filled with
discouragement
and strife.
A plan you make can
too often go astray,
but when we allow
God to direct our steps,
He keeps us steady,
and our hearts looking up,
as He guides us on our way.

If we trust
and put our faith in Him
Then He promises
That our lives will
abundantly overflow,
if we do not store up
Treasures on earth,
Where moth and rust
destroy, where thieves
break in and steal.

we can be sure
that where our treasure is,
there will our hearts be also,
and in so doing
we will certainly be
blessed beyond measure.

Jim Walkup
Revised 10-04-2017

Little One

My dearest little one,
if I could guard your heart
from all insensitivity and wrong
not leaving you wondering
what you could have done differently.
This is Pa Pa's wish for you,
That you alone are given
a special knowledge of
God's love which is given to some,
by those whose grace
continually overflows
out from rivers of living water
which has been given to a few.

Jim Walkup
12-12-2017

Outside 2

If a man looks at
the outside,
but God is concerned
with the heart,
you'll hear
people say that
beauty is only skin deep.
If you aren't
sure, then don't seek
understanding,
based simply on
what you can see.

If you look for God
in places far away
and forget
to acknowledge
the special place
where he lives
within the heart.
If you are not
seeking a way
you can be first
in his kingdom.

If you draw close
as little children
He promises to give
a blessed gentle space
where He tells us
we will discover
that His yoke is easy
and His burden is light
there we'll find
a special place,
a place within the heart,
a place of rest.

Jim Walkup
01-05-2018

Outside

If a man looks at
the outside,
but God is concerned
with the heart,
you'll hear
people say that
beauty is only skin deep.
If you aren't
sure, then don't seek
understanding,
based simply on
what you, yourself can see.

Jim Walkup
01-05-2018

Seeing A Child

is to love him.
Laughing with a man
is to know him.
Praying with a friend
is to understand him.

Jim Walkup
03-15-2018

I'm In Your Care

Seeing a child is to love him
Laughing with a man
is to understand him
Praying with a friend
is to know him.
When the climb is too steep
when hopes seem too dim
and my needs so great.
When I trust you, Lord
and look never to fate.
Will I be in awe
When to my knees
Suddenly, I fall.

When the numbness
In my legs seems far too
Great to bare
Do I cry out to you, Jesus
When my hurt I need to share
as I look up to the sky
And My path seems
not so clear
Do I fall down
to my knees
And know I'm in your care.

Jim Walkup
04-25-2018

Open Your Heart

To laugh with children
is to love them.
Praying with a special someone,
is to find joy.
Time spent with an,
old friend is to love him.
To share with someone is know them.

To open your heart is to find trust.
To share is to open your heart.
To listen is to walk the way,
and to simply display,
and be a real friend.

Jim Walkup
05- 28-2018

Harsh feelings

often run deep,
but forgiveness walks
a different, lighter
path when motivated by love.

Jim Walkup
08-17-2018

Thoughts 2

Never let bad thoughts
rule my mind and thinking.
Give all that you have
and love her dearly
the way she deserves.
Never let negative
thoughts rule your mind.
Learn to rejoice and treasure
the love you find
and give of your heart
in return.

Jim Walkup
08-28-2018

Seventy

If you have grown to be seventy
and are still rather young at heart,
without complaint.
I think then,
you've picked up a great
deal from this life and,
something most precious
from our creator God

Jim Walkup
03-25-2019

Finding Comfort

There is something really special
with holding another close,
nothing better than a warm
embrace between those
whom we love the most.

God created us to share
His love in this way,
at the end of a long day,
or a moment's fancy.

Finding comfort in each
other's arms, the strength
of embracing a loved one.
Only good can be found
in the touch of our embrace,
and pleasure within our reach.

Jim Walkup
06-01-2019

Contentment

It seems there will always
appear to be someone
faster stronger or smarter,
and possibly wiser,
so strive to look for
a place where you are
at peace and don't barter
for anything but instead
seek contentment.

Jim Walkup
06-11-2019

A Smile to My Heart

I was unlovable
and you put
your arms
around me, closely.

I felt unworthy
and your love
gave hope, encouragement,
and purpose from above.

I forgot how to sing
And your touch
caused my heart
to smile and bring
joy and eternal hope.

When I was sad
your word
made me glad
and brought a smile
to my heart.

Jim Walkup
08-28-2019

Poor In Spirit

If poor in spirit
You promise that mine
is the kingdom of heaven,
a pearl of great worth that shines
forth from the place
where every blessing flows.

Jim Walkup
03-22-2020

Treasure The Differences

One Important Thing
I've Learned in Life
That Brings
Special Joy
Is to Treasure the Differences
In the Person You Love.

Jim Walkup
05-07-2020

Rejoice in the LORD
(from Philippians 4:4-6)

You give me joy and my heart sings.
Rejoice in the LORD, gently rings
repeated again
I will say it again, rejoice.
A gentle reminder
be evident to all,
the Lord is near,
full of joy
confident and clear.
Do not be anxious about anything,
but in every situation bring,
a prayer and petition,
that rings
with thanksgiving,
a joyous condition
of the heart and mind,
remembering to present
your requests to God.

And the peace of God that
goes beyond understanding,
guards your hearts
and your minds in Christ Jesus,
And rejoices from the start.
Repeated again
And I will say it again, rejoice
A gentle reminder then,
let it be evident to all

Jim Walkup
07-27-2020

When you are Down

When you are DOWN to nothing
God is UP to something!
Seeing purpose and believing
when you have one of those days
where it simply gives you pause.
Faith sees the invisible,
Believes the laudable
In spite of inference that you may
See, even this will pass
going through what looks impossible.

You find no joy in the mark of stings
and arrows that find their mark.
It's not easy to be grateful
for the little things which seem over rated
know that our God offers us When you are DOWN
a way around
the worst circumstances or difficult days.
The things that seem doubtful
Can give way to something better.
Know that many have walked the fated
path, and the path that you walk can be
true, straight, and narrow.

Jim Walkup
11-14-2020

Standing In My Savior's Love

I found myself living a most
pleasant life in retirement,
knowing I've been given hope
and that I'm standing
in my Savior's love.
Wages cannot pay the price I owe
forgiven is an amazing word,
a blessing from my Holy LORD
Standing in my Savior's love.

Jim Walkup
3- 20- 2021

CPSIA information can be obtained
at www.ICGtesting.com
Printed in the USA
LVHW030802010621
689025LV00018B/1246